STAY

A practical guide to finishing what matters

Bart Traynor

Introduction

Most people don't quit when things are unbearable.

They quit when things are merely uncomfortable—when the effort outpaces the immediate reward, and no one is watching closely enough to notice.

That's the moment this book is about.

Not a crisis.

Not collapse.

The long middle—where responsibility continues, energy fades, and quitting would make sense.

There will always be a fire.

Not the kind that threatens—the kind that warms.

The kind you can stop beside and tell yourself you've done enough.

It will be reasonable.

It will make sense

This book isn't about never wanting the fire.

It's about recognising the moment you're standing near it.

I didn't learn this in a single defining event.

I learned it slowly—through discomfort I could no longer avoid, through responsibility I could no longer outsource, and through the quiet realisation that staying is not a personality trait.

It's a skill.

This is not a motivation book.

It won't promise transformation.

It won't offer shortcuts.

It won't tell you that you're capable of anything if you want it badly enough.

What it will do is help you understand:

- why quitting so often feels logical
- why preparation is an act of self-respect
- why discomfort lies about danger
- and how to stay present when others rely on you to remain steady

The stories here come from endurance racing, but this is not a sports book.

The lessons belong to anyone who carries responsibility quietly and cannot afford to fall apart easily.

If you're looking for inspiration, this may be a disappointment.

If you're looking for something steadier—something honest, practical, and quietly confronting—you're in the right place.

Why OCR? (And Why the Fire is Always Warm)

People often ask me why I do obstacle course racing. Not politely, either. Usually, it's delivered with a head tilt and a look that says, You're a clinical psychologist. You should know better.

They see the photos: mud, bruises, rope burns, and the odd bloody shin. They hear words like twenty-four hours, penalty loops, and ice baths. They imagine misery. Discomfort. Voluntary suffering.

And honestly, they're not wrong.

But they're missing the point.

OCR didn't teach me how to suffer. Life had already done that. OCR taught me how to stay when suffering showed up—how to not immediately reach for comfort, distraction, or an excuse.

Because for a long time, that's precisely what I did.

The Problem with Being Comfortable

For years, I lived under the quiet assumption that if something was uncomfortable, it probably wasn't worth sticking with. Not consciously. Not dramatically. Just subtly.

I wasn't lazy. I wasn't weak. I was capable enough at most things, which meant I always had options. And options are dangerous when discomfort arrives.

If a sport hurt, I found another one.

If something challenged my identity, I reframed it.

If commitment got heavy, I lightened the load— usually by walking away.

I didn't think of myself as a quitter. Quitters, I believed, gave up on everything. I gave up selectively. Strategically. Respectably.

Or so I told myself.

OCR stripped that story bare.

Why the Mud Works

Obstacle course racing is beautifully honest. It doesn't care about your intentions, your job title, or how good your excuses sound in your own head.

The wall is the height it is.

The rope is just as slippery.

The carry doesn't get lighter because you've had a hard week.

And the clock? The clock is ruthless.

There's no negotiating with an obstacle. You either get over it, through it, or you don't. If you don't, you wear the consequence—usually immediately.

That's why OCR works as a teacher. It removes the grey areas where most of us hide.

Life has plenty of loopholes. OCR does not.

Three Types of Obstacles (And Why This Matters)

It didn't take long for me to notice that obstacles fell into three clear categories.

Some you must complete alone. No one can lift your body weight for you. No one can hang onto the rope on your behalf. You either do the work or you don't.

Some you cannot complete alone. Walls, deep mud pits, moments of genuine exhaustion. These require another human being—not to rescue you, but to assist.

And some obstacles become classrooms. One lap, you need help. The next lap, you're the one offering it. That transition—from needing assistance to being able to give it—quietly rewires something in you.

Life works the same way. We pretend it doesn't.

We overestimate what we should do alone and underestimate when it's appropriate to ask for help. OCR doesn't let you hide from either mistake.

Night Falls, and the Fire Appears

Every twenty-four-hour race has a moment where the novelty wears off.

The crowd thins. The music fades. The sun drops. The temperature follows it. Your body starts to feel like it belongs to someone else.

And then there's the fire.

It's usually set up near the pit area—warm, crackling, inviting. Volunteers sit around it. Other racers stop there longer than necessary. The fire doesn't shout. It whispers.

You've done enough.

You've proven something already.

No one would judge you for stopping now.

At about two a.m., this conversation becomes very convincing.

Why Quitting Makes
Sense at Two a.m.

This is the part people don't talk about enough: quitting often feels logical, not weak.

At two a.m., your brain is exhausted. Your body is sore. Your emotional bandwidth is gone. The future shrinks to the next ten minutes.

This is where your mind starts lying—but politely.

You could rest and come back stronger next year.

Pushing through this isn't smart.

You've got responsibilities.

What's the point, really?

And here's the dangerous part: every one of those thoughts sounds reasonable.

This isn't panic. It's a negotiation.

The First Lie Fatigue Tells You

Fatigue doesn't scream. It reframes.

It tells you the story isn't worth finishing.

It tells you that stopping is wisdom.

It tells you that comfort is care.

But here's what OCR taught me: the first lie fatigue tells you is that this moment is permanent.

It isn't.

Energy returns. Pain changes. Dawn comes. But only if you stay.

The Skill of Staying

Staying is a skill. Not a personality trait. Not toughness. Not grit.

A skill.

And like any skill, it can be trained.

For me, staying often looked very unglamorous. Shortening my goals. Walking when I needed to. Singing stupid songs under my breath. Counting steps. Saying, just this obstacle. Just this lap.

Once—more than once—that song was Ice Ice Baby.

Not because it's inspirational. Because it has a beat. And sometimes, a beat is enough.

What the Fire Taught Me About Life

That fire shows up everywhere.

It shows up in relationships when they get hard.

It shows up at work when effort stops being rewarded immediately.

It shows up in health when progress slows.

The fire always offers the same thing: relief without growth.

OCR taught me that the goal isn't to never want the fire. The goal is to recognise the moment when the fire is speaking—and choose whether you're listening to fatigue or values.

Sometimes, stopping is the right call—wisdom matters.

But most of the time? Most of the time, stopping is just comfort dressed up as self-care.

And I had lived there long enough.

Why I Keep Coming Back

I don't race to prove I'm tough. I race to practise staying.

I race to remind myself that discomfort is survivable, that fatigue lies, and that I don't need to obey every thought I have.

I race because each time I walk past the fire, something quiet but solid grows.

And that thing follows me home.

The Question That Matters

At two a.m., standing near the fire, I always ask myself the same question:

If I stop now, will I be proud of the reason tomorrow?

Not proud of the outcome. Proud of the reason.

That question has saved me more times than motivation ever has.

Reflection

Where is your fire right now?
What is it offering you relief from?
And what would staying—just a little longer—
teach you?

Confessions of a
Comfortable Quitter

I didn't think of myself as a quitter.

That's important to say up front, because most people who struggle with commitment don't walk around wearing that label. Quitters, in my mind, were dramatic. They stormed off. They burned bridges. They gave up loudly.

I did it quietly.

Respectably.

I exited things with reasons.

Being "Good Enough" Is a Dangerous Place to Live

For most of my early life, I was capable of avoiding confronting my limits. I could do well without doing everything. I could succeed without fully committing. And because of that, I never had to sit for long with the discomfort of not knowing if I was good enough.

I had options.

Options sound like freedom, but they can quietly hollow you out.

When something got hard, I could pivot. When something demanded more than I wanted to give, I could redirect my attention. There was always another lane, another interest, another justification that sounded reasonable if you didn't look too closely.

The problem wasn't that I failed at things.

The problem was that I didn't stay long enough to find out who I might become if I did.

ADFA: Where the Story Started to Crack

Straight out of school, I was accepted into the Australian Defence Force Academy.

On paper, it was impressive. Competitive entry. Clear pathway. A future that made sense to other people.

On the ground, it was something else entirely.

Early mornings that blurred into late nights. A constant undercurrent of pressure. Physical exhaustion layered on top of mental strain. No space to negotiate. No space to opt out quietly.

And that's where the discomfort really began.

Not the yelling. Not the training. Not even the lack of sleep.

It was the realisation that I couldn't soften this experience to suit myself.

The Knee That Became an Exit

I had an old knee injury. It flared up during training.

Now, to be clear: the injury was real. The pain was real. The medical advice mattered.

But so did the relief.

When I was given leave to recover, something in me exhaled in a way that should have concerned me. The pressure lifted. The decision was no longer mine. I didn't have to decide whether to stay or go.

The knee decided for me.

At least, that's how I told the story.

I never returned.

For years afterward, I explained that moment with logic and hindsight. Para-infantry wasn't realistic. The injury would have held me back. It was the sensible call.

All of that might even be true.

But it wasn't the whole truth.

The Truth I Didn't Want to Admit

What I didn't say out loud—not then, not for a long time—was that ADFA demanded something I hadn't yet learned how to give: sustained discomfort without an immediate payoff.

There was no applause for sticking around. No reassurance that it would all make sense soon. Just repetition, fatigue, and the quiet expectation that you would keep turning up.

I told myself I was choosing wisely.

What I was really doing was choosing familiarity over growth.

And once you learn that you can exit discomfort with a good enough explanation, you start using that skill everywhere.

How Quitting Gets Smarter Over Time

The thing about quitting is that it evolves.

Early on, it's obvious. You walk away because something is hard.

Later, it becomes sophisticated. You walk away because something is "no longer aligned," or because "the timing isn't right," or because "there are other priorities."

Again—sometimes those things are true.

But sometimes they're just better language for the same old reflex.

Avoid prolonged discomfort.

The Cost of an Optional Life

For years after ADFA, I lived what I now think of as an optional life.

Nothing trapped me. Nothing forced me to stay. Nothing demanded that I dig in when things got uncomfortable.

That sounds enviable.

It wasn't.

Because without pressure, there's no reason to develop staying power. And without staying power, confidence becomes fragile. It depends on conditions remaining favourable.

I didn't lack ability.

I lacked proof—proof that I could remain present when things stopped being comfortable.

That proof matters later, when other people depend on you.

Responsibility Changes the Stakes

There comes a point in life where your decisions stop being entirely your own.

People rely on you. Not dramatically. Not always visibly. But consistently.

They rely on you to show up.

To not disappear when things are heavy.

To tolerate discomfort without immediately offloading it.

You don't rise to that responsibility in the moment. You rise—or fall—to the habits you've already built.

And at that point in my life, my habits leaned toward exit.

Why OCR Felt Different

Obstacle course racing didn't feel like another interest to sample. It felt like a confrontation.

There was no elegant way out mid-race. No narrative spin. No reframing that made stopping feel noble.

You either stayed or you didn't.

And for the first time in a long time, I wanted to stay —not because I was confident, but because I was tired of not knowing.

Tired of wondering how much of my potential I had quietly negotiated away.

The Question That Followed Me

There's a question I wish I had asked myself earlier in life:

Am I making this decision because it's right—or because it's relieving?

Relief feels good. But it doesn't always build anything.

OCR didn't magically fix my relationship with discomfort. It simply stopped allowing me to hide from it.

And once you've had that mirror held up to you, it's tough to unsee.

Reflection

23

Where in your life have you become very good at exiting—politely, logically, convincingly?

And what might happen if, just once, you stayed long enough to find out what's on the other side?

The Day I Couldn't
Hold My Daughter

24

Some moments don't arrive with drama.

They don't announce themselves as turning points.

They slip in quietly, then refuse to leave.

This was one of those moments.

A Small, Ordinary Task

It was a typical day. No crisis. No warning signs. Just the routine chaos that comes with caring for a newborn.

I leaned over the bath to lift my daughter.

She was tiny. Fragile. Entirely dependent.

And my back went.

Not a sharp crack. Not a cinematic collapse. Just a sudden, overwhelming failure of something I had always assumed would work when needed.

Pain shot through me, but that wasn't the worst part.

The worst part was the fear.

The Fear You Don't Expect

I couldn't straighten up. I couldn't adjust my grip. I couldn't trust my own body to do what it had done a thousand times before.

And for a split second, an obvious thought cut through everything else:

I might drop her.

That thought doesn't arrive gently. It hits hard and fast, and shame follows almost immediately.

I had to call out for help.

Standing there, bent awkwardly over the bath, I felt exposed in a way I hadn't before. Not physically—psychologically.

This wasn't about pain.

This wasn't about injury.

This was about identity.

When Capability Collapses

Up until that point, I had lived with an unspoken assumption: when it mattered, I would be able to cope.

That assumption had never been appropriately tested.

Suddenly, it was.

I wasn't just uncomfortable. I wasn't just struggling. I was unreliable at a time when reliability was non-negotiable.

That lands differently.

The Quiet Questions That Follow

The moment passed. Help arrived. My daughter was fine.

Life moved on.

But something inside me didn't.

In the days that followed, I kept returning to the same questions:

What if this happens again?

What if next time I'm alone?

What version of myself am I actually building?

Not the version I liked to imagine.

The version my habits were creating.

Responsibility Isn't About Strength

We tend to think responsibility is about being strong.

It isn't.

It's about being reliable under pressure.

It's about tolerating discomfort long before a crisis forces the issue. About preparing not for comfort, but for competence.

In that moment, I realised something uncomfortable: I had optimised my life for ease, not resilience.

And ease doesn't hold much weight when someone else is in your arms.

The Cost of
Deferred Discomfort

For years, I had postponed discomfort. Not dramatically. Not irresponsibly.

Just enough.

Enough to avoid structured training.

Enough to justify letting fitness slide.

Enough to stay within familiar limits.

It hadn't felt reckless at the time.

Standing there, it suddenly did.

A Decision, not a Promise

I didn't make a dramatic vow that day.

I didn't swear never to be weak again. I didn't commit to extremes. I didn't chase motivation.

I made a quieter decision.

I decided I would stop outsourcing my future capability to hope.

Hope that nothing would go wrong.

Hope that I'd rise when needed.

Hope that good intentions would be enough.

They aren't.

Becoming Someone Others Can Rely On

Responsibility doesn't always announce itself as parenthood.

Sometimes it looks like leadership.

Sometimes it looks like care work.

Sometimes it looks like being the person who doesn't disappear when things get heavy.

Whatever form it takes, the requirement is the same.

You don't get to fall apart easily.

Not because you're not allowed to struggle—but because other people shouldn't have to carry the cost of your avoidance.

That realisation changes how you train, how you plan. How you tolerate discomfort when no one is watching.

Why This Moment Matters

That day didn't make me tougher.

It made me honest.

Honest about the gap between who I thought I was and who I was actually prepared to be when it counted.

OCR came later. Training came later. Discipline came later.

But the decision started there—quietly, painfully, without applause.

The Work That No One Sees

Resilience doesn't start in emergencies.

It starts in ordinary moments, where no one is watching, and comfort is available.

That's where you choose whether to do the boring work. The unglamorous work. The work that doesn't feel urgent yet.

That's where you decide whether you're building a body—and a mind—that can be trusted.

Reflection

Who relies on you—directly or indirectly?

And if nothing changed, would the version of yourself you're building now be enough when it mattered?

Plan, Prepare, Then Shut Up and Trust

Most people think planning is about control.

It isn't.

It's about respect—for the task, for the process, and for the version of yourself who will have to perform when conditions aren't kind.

I learned this the slow way.

The Illusion of "Winging It"

For a long time, I liked to believe I performed best when things were loose. Flexible. Unstructured.

I told myself structure dulled creativity. That too much planning meant pressure. That I didn't want to turn life into a spreadsheet.

That story felt good.

It also gave me cover for something else: inconsistency.

If I didn't plan, I couldn't fail to follow the plan.

If I didn't prepare properly, I could always say I hadn't really committed.

If things went poorly, I had an explanation ready.

Winging it protects your ego. It does nothing for your results.

Preparation Is Boring —That's the Point

OCR is unforgiving when it comes to preparation.

You don't notice preparation when it's done well. You notice its absence immediately.

Forgot to practice grip? The rope exposes you.

Didn't train nutrition? Your stomach turns on you at three a.m.

Skipped strength work? Carries feel personal.

Preparation isn't glamorous. It doesn't feel heroic. It doesn't generate stories worth telling.

It quietly removes unnecessary suffering.

And that matters.

Planning Is an Act of Kindness

Good planning isn't about predicting every outcome. It's about reducing avoidable friction.

It's asking:

What can I control?

What usually goes wrong?

What version of me will turn up when I'm tired?

Planning is a gift you give your future self—the tired one, the distracted one, the version carrying more responsibility than energy.

That version of you deserves support.

When Planning Becomes Fear

There's a line, though. And it's easy to cross.

At some point, planning stops being preparation and starts being avoidance. More research. More tweaking. More "just one more week" before starting.

That's not preparation. That's fear wearing a high-functioning disguise.

The question is simple:

Is this planning helping me act—or helping me delay?

If it's the second, it's time to move.

Trust Is the Hardest Part

Trust doesn't mean blind confidence.

It means knowing you've done enough to stop micromanaging yourself when it counts.

In races, the worst moments come when you start second-guessing:

Should I be going faster?

Did I train enough?

Did I mess this up?

Those questions don't improve performance. They drain it.

Trust is the discipline of stopping the conversation once the work is done.

Shut Up and Execute

This is the part people resist.

They want reassurance mid-race. Confirmation that they're doing it right. Permission to believe it will work out.

There is no such permission.

There is only execution.

You planned.

You prepared.

Now it's time to shut up and do the next thing.

Not everything.

Not the finish line.

Just the next obstacle.

What This Looks Like Outside Racing

This principle shows up everywhere responsibility exists.

In leadership, it looks like preparing conversations rather than improvising them emotionally.

In health, it looks like boring consistency instead of reactive fixes.

In care roles, it looks like building capacity before you're exhausted.

Preparation doesn't make things easy.

It makes them possible.

The Relief of Trust

There's a strange relief that comes when you trust your preparation.

You stop arguing with yourself.

You stop negotiating.

You stop scanning for exits.

You do what's required.

That relief is earned, not granted.

The Question That Cuts Through Noise

45

When I'm tempted to overthink mid-race, I come back to this:

Did I do the work I said I would do?

If the answer is yes, then the thinking stops.

If the answer is no, then the work begins—without drama, without self-punishment.

Either way, clarity returns.

Reflection

Where are you seeking reassurance instead of relying on preparation?

And what would change if you planned not for comfort, but for competence?

You are Where You Are
(Stop Negotiating with That)

There's a strange ritual that happens the night before a hard thing.

People say it quietly, usually to themselves.

I wish I'd trained more.

It sounds like honesty. It sounds reflective. It even sounds responsible.

Most of the time, it's none of those things.

It's a negotiation.

The Comfort of
the Almost-Excuse

Saying I wish I'd trained more does something very specific psychologically.

It creates distance.

If things go well, you will exceed expectations.

If things go poorly, you've already explained why.

Either way, your identity stays intact.

The problem is that this mindset keeps you half-present. You turn up physically, but you hold something back—effort, belief, commitment—just in case you need the excuse later.

OCR punishes this immediately.

Starting Points Don't Care About Feelings

On the start line, no one asks how ready you feel.

Your body doesn't care what you meant to do.

The course doesn't care about good intentions.

The clock doesn't negotiate.

You start from where you are.

That's it.

And once you accept that fully—without judgement, without story—something surprising happens: pressure drops.

Because you stop fighting reality.

Acceptance Is Not Approval

This is where people get confused.

Accepting your starting point is not the same as approving of it.

You can be disappointed and still be honest.

You can want better and still work with what you have.

You can aim high without pretending you're already there.

Acceptance is simply removing fiction from the equation.

How Negotiation Wastes Energy

When you don't accept where you are, you waste enormous energy on internal commentary.

You compare yourself to past versions.

You compare yourself to others.

You replay decisions you can't undo.

Meanwhile, the work waits.

I've seen people with less ability consistently outperform others because they stopped arguing with reality and started acting within it.

That's not optimism. That's efficiency.

The Moment I Learned
This the Hard Way

In one race, early on, I realised I wasn't moving as well as I'd hoped. My legs cramped and felt heavy. My pacing plan suddenly felt optimistic.

Old me would have spiralled.

Instead, I did something very unremarkable: I adjusted.

Shorter goals.

More walking.

Cleaner transitions.

Fuel on a stricter schedule.

I didn't lower my standards. I lowered my expectations of how I would meet them.

That distinction matters.

Where People Lose the Plot

People often mistake ambition for ignoring reality.

They assume that admitting fatigue, limits, or mistakes means lowering standards.

It doesn't.

Ignoring reality doesn't make you faster.

Honesty does.

Once you accept where you are, every decision becomes clearer:

- How hard can I push without breaking?
- What's the smartest next move?
- Where do I need help?

Those questions don't come from self-criticism.

They come from clarity.

Responsibility Changes This Equation

When others rely on you, negotiation becomes costly.

If you're responsible for a team, a family, or outcomes beyond yourself, pretending you're better prepared than you are doesn't help anyone.

Honesty becomes a form of care.

You plan differently.

You pace differently.

You ask for help sooner.

You stop gambling with other people's trust.

The Discipline of Saying "This Is It"

There's a discipline in saying:

This is my fitness.

This is my capacity.

This is my starting point.

No drama. No apology.

From there, the only meaningful question is:

What's the best use of what I have right now?

That question moves you forward.

The Freedom of the Present Moment

When you stop negotiating with reality, you become more effective in it.

You stop replaying the past.

You stop projecting failure into the future.

You deal with what's directly in front of you.

That's not resignation.

That's presence.

Reflection

Where are you still negotiating with your starting point?

And what might change if you committed fully to working with reality instead of arguing with it?

Know Your Why (Borrowed Motivation Fails Fast)

Motivation gets far more credit than it deserves.

People talk about it as if it's something you either have or don't. As if the right quote, podcast, or morning routine will summon it on demand.

That hasn't been my experience.

Motivation is unreliable. Purpose is not.

The Problem with
Borrowed Reasons

Early on, I borrowed my reasons.

I borrowed them from people I admired. From social media. From books written by people who looked far more disciplined than I felt.

I told myself I was training to be "better." To be "stronger." To "set a good example."

None of those are bad reasons.

They're just vague enough to disappear the moment discomfort shows up.

At two a.m., vague reasons don't survive.

Why Discomfort Is a Filter

Discomfort strips motivation down to what's real.

When you're tired, cold, or overwhelmed, you don't rise to your aspirations. You fall back to your values— the ones you've actually integrated, not just admired.

That's why some people keep going quietly while others, who sounded far more motivated, fall apart when conditions change.

Their why was cosmetic.

A Why That Needs
Applause Won't Last

One of the clearest lessons OCR taught me is this:

If your reason for doing something requires recognition, it won't survive isolation.

Night races make this obvious. There's no crowd. No one is filming. No one impressed.

If your why needs an audience, it evaporates in the dark.

The reasons that last are private. Often unremarkable. Sometimes uncomfortable to admit.

The Shift That
Made the Difference

At some point, my why stopped being about achievement and started being about reliability.

Not proving anything.

Not impressing anyone.

Not chasing identity.

Just becoming someone who could be counted on—by others and by myself.

That shift changed everything.

Because reliability doesn't need to feel good in the moment, it just needs to be honoured.

Responsibility Clarifies Purpose

When other people depend on you, your why gets tested quickly.

Not in grand moments—in small ones.

Will you do the unglamorous work?

Will you manage your energy?

Will you tolerate inconvenience without passing it on?

Purpose becomes practical.

It stops being about meaning and starts being about behaviour.

The Why That Survives Fatigue

The why that survives isn't inspirational. It's grounding.

It sounds more like.

This is who I said I would be.

Someone relies on me being steady.

I don't want to explain why I didn't try.

Those reasons don't light you up.

They steady you.

And steadiness lasts.

When Motivation Disappears (And It Will)

Motivation always disappears eventually.

The mistake is treating that as a problem.

It isn't.

The absence of motivation is the signal that it's time to rely on commitment instead.

Commitment doesn't ask how you feel. It asks what you decided.

Borrow Less. Build More.

A strong why isn't discovered. It's built.

Built through repetition.

Through follow-through.

Through choosing discomfort when it aligns with who you want to be.

Over time, that creates something motivation never can: trust.

Trust that you'll show up even when the feeling doesn't.

The Question Worth Asking

67

When things get hard, ask yourself this:

Is my reason strong enough to keep me company when no one is watching?

If the answer is no, don't panic.

Refine it.

Because borrowed motivation is cheap—and it fails fast.

Reflection

What are you relying on to keep you going right now—
inspiration or identity?

And if motivation disappeared tomorrow, what would
still matter enough to continue?

Get Out of Your Head
(Your Brain Quits First)

If you spend enough time doing hard things, you learn something unsettling:

Your brain will try to stop you long before your body actually needs to.

Not dramatically.

Not hysterically.

Politely. Rationally. Convincingly.

And if you don't recognise what's happening, you'll believe every word of it.

The Day Everything
Was "Broken"

During one long race, I came into the pit convinced I was injured.

Not sore. Not tired. Injured.

My shin felt sharp and unstable. The kind of pain that makes you start building a story around it. I was certain something was wrong, fractured. I told myself it would be irresponsible to continue, but I pushed.

Twenty kilometres later, the shin had settled.

Now it was my hip.

Later still, my knee.

By the end of the race, I had a rotating cast of body parts, all apparently one bad decision away from permanent damage.

A month later, nothing was broken.

What had been broken was my ability to interpret signals accurately while exhausted.

Fatigue Is a Terrible Narrator

Fatigue doesn't just make things harder. It changes how you interpret what's happening.

Pain feels more threatening.

The effort feels less effective.

The future feels closer and darker.

This isn't a weakness. It's biology.

When you're tired, your brain shifts into protection mode. It scans for threats. It becomes conservative. It wants you safe, warm, and still.

That's useful if you're actually in danger.

It's unhelpful if you're simply uncomfortable.

The Brain's Favourite Trick

The brain's most effective strategy isn't panic.

It's persuasion.

It tells you:

This pain means something is wrong.

Continuing would be stupid.

You can always come back another day.

Each thought sounds reasonable on its own.

Together, they form a very convincing argument for stopping.

The problem is that arguments built under fatigue rarely reflect reality.

Pain, Discomfort, and Actual Danger

One of the most useful distinctions I've learned is this:

Not all pain means stop.

Some pain means adjust.

Some pain means slow down.

Some pain means pay attention.

Very little pain means abandon everything immediately.

The skill isn't ignoring pain.

The skill is interpreting it accurately.

And that skill disappears first when you're tired.

Why Arguing with Thoughts Doesn't Work

A common mistake is trying to reason your way out of these moments.

You start debating yourself:

But I trained for this.

But other people are still going.

But I'll regret quitting.

That usually makes things worse.

Because now you're tired and mentally busy.

The goal isn't to win an argument with your thoughts.

It's to stop giving them the microphone.

Naming Beats Negotiating

One of the simplest tools I use is naming what's happening.

This is fatigue talking.

This is discomfort, not danger.

This is the moment my brain always tries this.

Naming doesn't remove the sensation.

It removes its authority.

Once you label the thought, you create just enough distance to choose your response rather than obey it.

Shrinking the Horizon

Another trap fatigue sets is expanding the task.

Your brain jumps straight to the finish line. Or the remaining hours. Or everything that still needs to be done.

That's overwhelming and unnecessary.

I've learned to shrink the horizon aggressively.

Not finish the race.

Just get to the next obstacle.

Not another six hours.

Just ten more minutes.

Your brain copes better with what's close.

When Stopping Is Actually the Right Call

This matters: sometimes stopping is the right decision.

The skill isn't never stopping.

The skill is knowing why you're stopping.

Are you stopping because something is genuinely wrong—or because your brain is tired of being uncomfortable?

Those reasons feel similar in the moment. They are very different afterward.

The Test I Come Back To

When I'm unsure, I ask myself this:

If I stop now, will I be proud of the reason tomorrow?

Not proud of the outcome.

Proud of the reason.

That question cuts through fatigue better than motivation ever has.

This Shows Up Everywhere

You don't need to run an ultra to experience this.

This mental pattern shows up:

in difficult conversations

in leadership decisions

in health habits

in caregiving roles

The brain tries to protect you from discomfort by reducing effort.

Sometimes that's wise.

Often, it's just familiar.

Learning to Stay
Mentally Present

Getting out of your head doesn't mean becoming fearless.

It means becoming less obedient to every thought that passes through when you're tired.

It means noticing the story without becoming it.

That's not toughness.

That's skill.

Reflection

When things get hard, what does your brain usually try to convince you of?

And how often do you mistake discomfort for danger?

When Thinking
Turns Against You

Early in a race, thinking is useful.

You monitor pace.

You check form.

You adjust strategy.

Later, thinking turns into commentary.

This is taking too long.

Why does everything hurt?

I should be further along by now.

None of those thoughts helps you move forward. They just consume energy.

That's when it's time to stop thinking altogether.

Give Your Brain a Beat

There comes a point in every hard effort where thinking becomes the problem.

You're not confused.

You're not unmotivated.

You're just overloaded.

At that point, asking your brain to solve anything is a bad idea.

It doesn't need more information.

It needs something simpler.

Why Rhythm Works

Rhythm gives your brain a job that doesn't involve judgement.

Counting steps.

Matching breath to movement.

Repeating a phrase.

It occupies the mental space that fatigue would otherwise fill with doubt.

This isn't motivation.

It's management.

The Day a Ridiculous
Song Saved Me

At some point during a long overnight race—cold, dark, and deeply unimpressive—my brain refused to cooperate.

Every step felt heavy. Every obstacle felt unnecessary. I wasn't injured. I wasn't in danger.

I was just done.

So, I stopped trying to reason with myself and started repeating a song.

Ice Ice Baby.

Not quietly. Not proudly. But rhythmically.

Step. Step. Breath.

Ice. Ice. baby.

It had a beat.

That was enough.

Why This Isn't as Silly as It Sounds

From a psychological perspective, rhythm does three important things:

1) It narrows attention.

Your brain stops scanning for problems and focuses on cadence.

2) It regulates breathing.

Steady breath reduces perceived effort.

3) It interrupts rumination.

You can't catastrophise and count at the same time.

You don't need insight in those moments.

You need momentum.

Create Your Own Beat

Create Your Own Beat

The content doesn't matter.

It can be:

a phrase

a lyric

a count

a nonsense sound

What matters is that it's:

simple

repeatable

steady

If it makes you smile, even better. Humour breaks tension faster than seriousness ever has. Another rhythm that's carried me through complete fatigue is this one:

Fast feet, legs strong —

I can do this all night long.

It's simple. It has cadence. And it tells your body exactly what to do without asking your brain for permission.

There's nothing profound about it—and that's the point.

When you're exhausted, you don't need inspiration. You need instructions that your body can follow automatically. Short phrases like this give direction without debate. They bypass overthinking and return you to movement.

I've used it when everything felt heavy, and progress felt painfully slow. Not because I believed I could actually go "all night long," but because repeating it kept me moving.

And right now, is always enough.

This Works Off the Course Too

This isn't an OCR trick.

People use rhythm to:

get through tough conversations

manage anxiety

stay present under pressure

push through fatigue in daily responsibilities

Any time your thoughts are noisy, rhythm gives you a way out without confrontation.

Stop Trying to Be Impressive

There's a strange pressure to respond to difficulty with depth.

Profound thoughts. Big insights. Meaningful reframes.

Sometimes the most effective response is just putting one foot in front of the other with a beat that keeps you moving.

That's not shallow.

That's practical.

When the Beat
Carries You Through

Eventually, something shifts.

The beat fades.

Movement feels lighter.

Thinking becomes optional again.

You didn't solve anything.

You stayed.

And sometimes, that's the entire victory.

Reflection

92

When thinking makes things worse, what could you
replace it with?

And what simple rhythm might help you keep moving
when effort feels heavy?

Comparison is the Fastest Way to Bleed Energy

There's nothing wrong with noticing other people.

The problem starts when noticing turns into measuring.

In OCR, that mistake gets expensive very quickly.

How Comparison Sneaks In

It rarely arrives as envy.

It shows up as curiosity.

They look smoother than me.

They're moving faster.

They seem less affected.

Those thoughts don't feel toxic. They feel observational.

But once you start running someone else's race in your head, your own effort loses clarity.

Why Watching
Others Drains You

Comparison does something subtle yet powerful: it pulls your attention away from your body and toward outcomes you don't control.

You stop listening to your breath.

You stop noticing your pacing.

You stop responding to your own signals.

Instead, you try to match someone else's rhythm, strength, or strategy—usually without knowing their background, their training, or their limits.

That's how people blow up.

Borrowed Strategies
Break Weekend Warriors

Elite athletes can afford risks that others can't.

They recover faster.

They tolerate higher loads.

They've trained specifically for their style.

Copying them without context isn't ambitious. It's careless.

I learned this early on. Watching stronger or faster competitors and trying to follow them cost me more than they ever gained me. I paid in fatigue, mistakes, and frustration.

My best races started when I stopped trying to look like someone else and started moving in a way I could sustain.

Energy Is Finite— Spend It Wisely

Every comparison costs something.

It costs focus.

It costs presence.

It costs trust in your own process.

That might not matter early on.

Later, when energy is scarce, it matters a lot.

Your Race Is
Quiet for a Reason

There's a moment in long events when the field spreads out.

You don't see many people.

You don't hear encouragement.

You just move.

That quiet is deliberate.

It removes distraction. It forces you inward.

That's where you either settle into your own pace—or unravel trying to imagine how everyone else is doing.

Responsibility Changes the Metric

When others rely on you, comparison becomes even less useful.

You're not competing for validation.

You're building capacity.

You're modelling steadiness.

Trying to be someone else under pressure doesn't just drain you—it creates instability for the people around you.

Consistency matters more than appearance.

What "Just Do You" Actually Means

This phrase gets thrown around casually.

What it really means is:

Trust your preparation.

Respect your limits.

Commit to your process.

Stop borrowing pressure.

Doing you isn't about being special.

It's about being reliable.

The Discipline of Looking Away

One of the most effective skills I've learned is the discipline of looking away.

Away from pace charts.

Away from those who passed me.

Away from imaginary standings.

Back to breath.

Back to form.

Back to the next step.

That's where control lives.

The Quiet Wins

Some of the strongest performances I've seen never looked impressive.

They looked steady.

Uneventful.

Unremarkable.

And then, hours later, those people were still moving.

Comparison chases moments.

Commitment survives time.

Reflection

Where are you measuring yourself against someone else's path?

And what would change if you redirected that energy back into your own process?

Let Others Walk Beside You—Not Carry You

For a long time, I misunderstood support.

I thought needing help meant weakness.

I also thought asking for help meant handing responsibility over.

Both ideas turned out to be wrong.

The Mistake I Made Early On

Before one overnight winter race, I said something to my dad that I thought sounded committed.

"If I try to stop, don't let me."

It came from a good place. I wanted accountability. I wanted backup when things got hard.

What I was really doing, though, was outsourcing ownership.

I was handing someone else responsibility for a decision that could only ever be mine.

Why That Doesn't Work

When you give someone else the job of stopping you from quitting, two things happen.

First, you create pressure where support should live.

Second, you remove your own agency from the equation.

If you stop, it's their failure.

If you continue, it's their enforcement.

Neither is fair.

Support is meant to steady you, not steer you.

Ownership Can't Be Delegated

In OCR—and in life—there are decisions no one else can make for you.

No one can:

move your legs

hold your focus

decide to stay when it's uncomfortable

Others can encourage you.

They can remind you.

They can walk beside you.

But they can't carry the choice.

What Healthy Support Actually Looks Like

I've learned to be much clearer about the kind of support I need.

Not:

"Make me keep going."

But:

"Remind me why I'm here."

"Help me think clearly when I'm tired."

"Be steady when I wobble."

That shift changes everything.

It keeps responsibility where it belongs while still allowing connection.

The Strength of
Walking Together

Some of the most powerful moments in OCR happen quietly.

Someone matches your pace for a while.

You share a few words.

Then one of you moves on.

No drama. No rescue.

Just presence.

That kind of support doesn't weaken you. It reinforces you.

This Applies Beyond Racing

This lesson matters anywhere responsibility exists.

In leadership, it's the difference between delegation and abdication.

In care roles, it's the difference between support and burnout.

In relationships, it's the difference between partnership and dependency.

You can accept help without giving away agency.

That balance is learned, not assumed.

When You Become the One Who Walks Beside

Over time, roles shift.

The person who once helped you now needs support.

The one who struggled now steadies others.

OCR makes this visible. Life does too, if you're paying attention.

Being able to walk beside someone without carrying them is a skill worth developing.

It requires patience.

It requires boundaries.

It requires trust.

Responsibility Is Shared, Not Shifted

Support works best when responsibility is shared but not shifted.

You own your choices.

Others support your capacity to make them well.

That's not independence.

That's maturity.

The Question That Keeps Me Honest

Before asking for help now, I ask myself:

Am I asking for support—or am I asking to be relieved of responsibility?

The answer shapes the conversation.

Reflection

Where could support strengthen you without replacing your responsibility?

And how might you offer that kind of support to someone else?

Gratitude isn't Soft —It's a Weapon

Gratitude has a branding problem.

It's often presented as something gentle. Reflective. A nice add-on when things are already going well.

That version of gratitude doesn't help much when you're exhausted, frustrated, or carrying responsibility that doesn't let up.

The kind that works shows up under pressure.

When Gratitude
Actually Matters

Early in races, gratitude is easy.

You're fresh. People are encouraging. Everything still feels possible.

Later—when things are heavy, and progress is slow—gratitude feels irrelevant. Almost insulting.

That's exactly when it matters most.

Because at that point, gratitude stops being about feeling good and starts being about where you place your attention.

Gratitude as Practice, Not Personality

What OCR taught me about gratitude wasn't philosophical.

It was practical.

Early on, a close friend suggested something that sounded slightly ridiculous at the time:

Say thank you to every volunteer. And say thank you to the obstacles.

Out loud.

I tried it.

At first, it felt awkward. People around me probably thought I'd lost the plot. But something unexpected happened.

Saying thank you changed how I approached the next challenge.

Thanking the Obstacle

When you thank a challenging obstacle, you stop fighting it before you've even started.

You don't tense up.

You don't catastrophise.

You don't personalise the difficulty.

You meet it as something to engage with rather than something to resent.

"Thank you" sounds passive. It isn't.

It places you in a position of choice and presence. It turns the obstacle into a task rather than a threat.

And when you're tired, that distinction matters.

Volunteers and Perspective

The same thing happened with volunteers.

High-fiving. Saying thank you and making eye contact.

It pulled me out of my head and reminded me that this whole thing—as hard as it was—was supported. Chosen. Shared.

Gratitude stopped being a feeling and became a behaviour.

When the Habit
Followed Me Elsewhere

That habit stuck.

So much so that during a triathlon some time later, I saw a marshal ahead of me with his arm out.

Without thinking, I called out a big "Thank you!" and slapped his hand as I passed.

It was only from his stunned expression that I realised he wasn't offering a high five.

He was pointing in the direction we were supposed to go.

For a moment, I felt foolish.

Then I glanced back and saw him laughing with his colleague, both of them smiling.

Job done, I thought.

Why This Matters

Gratitude didn't make the race easier.

It made me more present.

More focused.

Less adversarial.

Less consumed by discomfort.

That's why it works.

Not because it softens the challenge—but because it sharpens your engagement with it.

Reflection

What would change if you met difficulty with appreciation rather than resistance?

And where could a simple thank you help you stay present when things get hard?

What Finishing Actually Means

Finishing rarely looks the way people imagine it will.

There's no slow-motion moment.

No swelling music.

No clear sense of arrival.

Most of the time, it's messy. Anti-climactic. Quiet.

And that's exactly why it matters.

The Myth of the Finish Line

We tend to think finishing will feel like resolution.

That crossing the line will tidy everything up, and the discomfort will suddenly make sense. That we'll feel different—lighter, clearer, transformed.

Sometimes there's relief.

Often there's just... stillness.

You stop moving. You breathe. You look around.

And then life continues.

Finishing Isn't About the Outcome

Over time, I've realised that finishing has very little to do with where you end up.

It's about how you behaved when quitting would have been easier.

Did you stay present?

Did you keep choosing the next step?

Did you hold your values when no one was watching?

Those questions matter long after the event fades.

The Quiet Repair That Happens Along the Way

Finishing doesn't fix you.

It repairs something subtler.

Each time you stay when it's uncomfortable, you rebuild trust in yourself. Quietly. Incrementally.

You stop wondering whether you'll disappear when things get hard.

That trust shows up later—in responsibility, in relationships, in leadership—often without you noticing.

Until you need it.

When Finishing
Looks Like Adjusting

Not every finish is clean.

Sometimes finishing means slowing down.

Sometimes it means changing the plan.

Sometimes it means accepting a version of success that looks different from what you imagined.

That's not failure.

That's maturity.

The people who last are the ones who adapt without abandoning themselves.

Responsibility Changes the Definition

When others rely on you, finishing takes on a different shape.

It's not about personal triumph.

It's about steadiness.

About being predictable in the best possible way.

Finishing becomes less about proving something and more about not passing the cost of discomfort on to others.

That's a different kind of strength.

The Work Continues
After the Line

The most important work doesn't happen at the finish line.

It happens the next morning.

In ordinary decisions.

In whether you carry forward what you practised.

Discomfort tolerance.

Honest self-assessment.

Gratitude under pressure.

The ability to stay.

Those don't retire when the race ends.

The Race You're Actually In

Most people reading this aren't training for OCRs or ultras.

They're navigating responsibility.

Fatigue.

Commitment.

The long middle of things that don't offer applause.

That is the race.

And the same rules apply.

What I Hope You Take with You

Not motivation.

Not inspiration.

Just a clearer relationship with discomfort.

An understanding that:

Staying is a skill

Preparation is self-respect

Gratitude is practical

Support doesn't remove responsibility

finishing is quieter than we expect—and more meaningful for it

A Final Thought

There will always be a fire.

Not the kind that threatens.

The kind that warms.

The kind you reach when you're tired enough, sore enough, or worn down enough that stopping feels reasonable. The kind that offers relief without judgement. The kind that asks very little of you.

And most of the time, no one would blame you for staying there.

That's what makes it dangerous.

People rarely quit because they can't continue.

They quit because continuing no longer feels necessary.

Because they've done enough.

Because they've proven enough.

Because no one is watching closely anymore.

The fire doesn't shout.

It doesn't rush you.

It simply waits.

What this book has tried to show is not that you should always push on.

Sometimes stopping *is* the right decision.

But there is a difference between stopping because you've chosen to—and stopping because you've drifted into comfort without noticing.

That difference is awareness.

Staying is not about toughness.

It's about clarity.

Clarity about why you're here.

Clarity about who relies on you.

Clarity about the quiet promises you've made—not to others, but to yourself.

Staying is the moment you recognise the fire for what it is, feel its warmth, and still decide deliberately what comes next.

For people carrying responsibility, this matters deeply.

Because quitting rarely looks dramatic.

It looks sensible.

It looks like rest.

It looks like "someone else can take it from here."

Sometimes that's true.

Sometimes it's just fatigue talking.

It's not about never stopping.

It's about knowing why you're stopping.

To finish things honestly.

To rest when it's chosen, not when it's leaked into.

To remain someone you can trust—especially when no one is asking you to.

There will always be a fire.

It's whether you recognise it

and choose to stay, calmly and deliberately,

long enough to finish what matters

and remain the person you intend to be.

Afterword

Most people don't quit when things are unbearable.

They quit when stopping feels reasonable.

Stay is a calm, confronting book for people who carry responsibility under pressure. Drawing on lessons from endurance racing, psychology, and everyday life, it explores what allows people to remain steady when fatigue, discomfort, and doubt make quitting make sense.

This is not a motivation book.

It's about clarity, preparation, and the quiet decision to stay long enough to finish what matters—and remain the person you intend to be.

About the Author

Bart is a straight-talking, passionate, and innovative Clinical Psychologist and operational leader with over 20 years' experience helping individuals, teams, and organisations thrive under pressure. He is known for making the complex simple, translating psychology into practical tools that work in real life, not just in theory.

With a particular interest in men's health, organisational culture, and performance psychology, Bart has delivered keynote presentations nationally and internationally. His work sits at the intersection of psychology, responsibility, and endurance, focusing less on motivation and more on the skills required to remain steady when others depend on you.

Through clinical practice, leadership, and endurance sport, he has become deeply interested in what allows people to *stay*—to remain present, reliable, and clear-headed when quitting would be understandable.

Above all, he is passionate about reshaping the conversation around mental health: moving it beyond crisis management and toward strength, clarity, and purposeful action in everyday life.

Bart is passionate about connecting with and learning from others. Whether you're interested in mental health, performance, exercise, leadership, or simply want to continue the conversation, he would love to hear from you.You can connect with Bart through the links below.

instagram.com/livebetterzone
linkedin.com/in/bart-traynor-1681039a

www.ingramcontent.com/pod-product-compliance
Lightning Source LLC
Chambersburg PA
CBHW031337060726
47590CB00007B/2505